The Troll Called Bill

AF585563

Maureen Haselhurst

Illustrated by Garry Parsons

The troll called Bill . . .

ran up the hill.

He got to the top . . .

Huff! Puff!

and saw Big Boss the Bull!

"Buzz off!" said Big Boss.

The troll called Bill
rolled back down the hill!